Tula PINK

COLORING *with* THREAD

STITCHING A *whimsical world* WITH HAND EMBROIDERY

Fons&Porter

fw

www.fwcommunity.com

21 20 19 18   5 4 3

Distributed in the U.K. and Europe by F&W MEDIA
INTERNATIONAL
Pynes Hill Court, Pynes Hill, Rydon Lane
Exeter, EX2 5AZ, United Kingdom
Tel: (+44) 1392 797680
E-mail: enquiries@fwmedia.com

SRN: R5336
ISBN-13: 978-1-4402-4811-5

EDITORIAL DIRECTOR: Kerry Bogert
EDITOR: Christine Doyle
TECHNICAL EDITOR: Deanna Hall West
ART DIRECTOR: Ashlee Wadeson
COVER AND INTERIOR DESIGNER: Karla Baker
ILLUSTRATOR: Sue Friend
PHOTOGRAPHER: George Boe &
Dean Schoeppner

contents

INTRODUCTION

For the last decade I have committed myself to designing fabric for the sewing community. Designing for fabric is a tricky thing as an artist because I don't control the final outcome of the piece. The fabrics that I design don't reach their full potential until someone picks up the fabric and makes something out of it, be that a quilt, a dress, a bag, or some other fabric-based project. As artists, we are taught to see our vision through to the end, to consider every detail, and to be intentional and meaningful at every step. I have entrusted my work into the hands of others, some friends and many more complete strangers. I have always viewed this process as the ultimate collaboration, and I have never been disappointed by the creativity of those silent collaborators. I see hundreds of images scroll across my Instagram feed from people I have never met doing incredible things with my fabrics. They use my fabrics in ways that go so far beyond the reaches of my single mind. I am humbled and delighted by this day after day.

A few years ago I took those images so lovingly created for fabric and drained them of color, reduced them to lines, and handed those illustrations over, yet again, to be interpreted by people in the form of a coloring book. To my insane delight, people rose to the challenge

and filled those pages with vibrant color and almost made me jealous of my own work. This experiment of starting a creative thought and handing it over to the world to be completed by hands that I have never met has become the most crucial part of my process. Perhaps more importantly, I feel connected so deeply to the creative process of thousands of others. I can barely wrap my mind around the enormity of this global collaboration.

When it came time to take those illustrations and put them together in the form of hand embroidery, there was only one path to take in my mind. I opened the project up to the vast knowledge of the community that has handled my work with so much love and respect, the community that has been my silent partner for all of these years. I put out a call for creative talent to take my beloved drawings and interpret them in thread. The response was overwhelming, and the fruits of that labor can be found on the pages that follow. Talented hand stitchers from all over answered that call, and with little more than a line drawing and few skeins of floss, they breathed new life into my illustrations.

Now it's your turn. Using the stitch guide and motifs in these pages, load your needle with colorful thread and collaborate with me.

I am forever grateful to the following stitchers and their seemingly endless cache of talent for helping to make this book a reality:

ELISE BAEK
JENNA J. BEEGLE
JESSE COTTRELL
CAROLINE DAIGLE
TRACEY DENNISTON
WENDY DUNHAM
LISA GUNNUFSEN
ELIZABETH HILL
CHARLENE HEARST
TESSA HUTCHINSON
NYDIA KEHNLE
ANNETTE MILLARD
KATE PIETSCHMAN
JODIE RACKLEY
HANNAH ROBINSON
JANICE SIMMONS
PAT SMITH
EMILY VARDEMAN
REBECCA J. VENTON
NICHOLE VOGELSINGER
ANGELA ZOLNER

GETTING STARTED

Before beginning to stitch the designs, let's review some embroidery basics.

FABRIC

The designs in this book are stitched on a variety of colors and types of fabric. The only limitation on the type of fabric selected is that you must be able to poke your needle through it easily. Beyond that, the sky's the limit! Here are some common choices.

Quilting cotton: This is a lightweight woven fabric that comes in a huge array of colors and prints. Solid cottons will always work, but consider a light print for some of the designs, too. Tone-on-tone and low-volume prints work well. If the fabric is very lightweight, add a layer of stabilizer material to the back of the fabric for easier stitching.

Linen: Like quilting cotton, linen is a woven fabric that ranges from lightweight to medium-weight. It has more texture than quilting cotton, which adds interest to the designs. When the linen is of a lighter weight, it's best for the designs to be of a lighter, airier nature rather than selecting very dense designs. If the linen is heavier, it can be used for home decor projects such as pillows.

Canvas: The heaviest of the most common fabrics is canvas. It, too, is woven, but it's so heavy it can sometimes be difficult to pass a needle through it. If you have trouble, try using a thimble or rubber needle puller.

Felt: A nonwoven fabric, felt comes in a range of colors and thicknesses. It's loftier than the woven choices, and it won't bunch up if you make tight

tip

To find the center of the fabric, fold the fabric twice from edge to edge and mark the point where the fold lines intersect with a pin, chalk, or thread tack.

stitches. Because it's lofty, you'll need to use several strands of floss or thicker thread so the stitches don't get lost or buried in the felt.

Whatever fabric you use, cut the piece to be at least 2" (5 cm) larger than the design on all sides.

THREAD

All the designs in this book were stitched with Anchor embroidery floss. **Embroidery floss** is usually made from cotton, is widely available, and comes in a huge array of colors. Most embroidery floss is composed of six individual strands. The individual strands pull apart easily so you can change the look of the stitches: one strand will produce fine and lacy stitches; six strands will produce bold, dense stitches; and three strands (a common number) will fall in between.

There are metallic and rayon flosses available, as well as some in neon (a few are used in this book) and even glow-in-the-dark colors.

Separate the strands of embroidery floss one at a time, and then recombine the desired number of strands.

If you're feeling more adventurous, there are other thread options to consider. **Pearl cotton** is made of twisted strands, but unlike embroidery floss, they don't separate. Therefore, it's important that you buy the right thread thickness for your project; size 8 is a fairly typical weight for embroidery. **Yarn, crochet thread,** and **crewel thread** are all on the heavy side, so you likely won't complete an entire design with them, but they could add an interesting texture to French knots or some other individual stitches.

TOOLS

Now that you have your materials chosen, let's talk tools.

Needle: Embroidery needles are made specifically for the task at hand. They have a large eye, making it easier to thread multiple strands of floss. Longer needles work well for running stitches (see Stitch Guide), while you may find that shorter needles are better for making French knots (see Stitch Guide). If using a very loosely woven fabric, a tapestry needle with its very large eye and blunt point is an option.

Scissors: Any scissors type will do, but it's nice to have a couple of specific scissors at the ready. Fabric scissors are large and handy for cutting all the types of fabrics. Small, pointed embroidery scissors are best for trimming and removing threads.

Seam ripper: Speaking of removing threads, there will be times when your stitches don't turn out quite the way you'd hoped. They're part of the wonderful imperfection of something handmade. However, if you want to remove them, a seam ripper will make quick and easy work of the task.

Embroidery hoop: Placing your fabric in an embroidery hoop (or a scroll or snap-together frame, which are better for the heavier-weight fabrics) pulls the fabric taut, preventing it from bunching up as you stitch. Some people prefer to embroider in a hoop or frame, while others prefer to feel the fabric and thread in their hands while they stitch. The choice is yours, so do whatever works best for you. Hoops are available in wood, metal, or plastic and in many shapes and sizes; scroll and snap frames are a bit more limited. A word of caution: Be sure to keep the fabric grainlines perpendicular to each other to prevent eventual puckers and folds with the stitches.

ACCESSING THE CD CONTENT

The designs are provided to you on the CD in the back of this book. Although it is recommended that you use Adobe Acrobat Reader 9 to view the disk content, your computer may be set up to open PDF files in a different application by default. If your computer does not have an application to view PDF files, you can get the latest version of the free Adobe Acrobat Reader from the Adobe website: http://get.adobe.com/reader/. Simply type this URL into your browser's address bar.

TRANSFER METHODS

So, how do you get the chosen design onto the fabric? Here are a few options.

Tracing method: Trace the design directly onto the fabric, using a pencil, dressmaker's chalk, or an embroidery marker. Place the fabric over the printed design and trace the design onto the fabric. If you're having trouble seeing the design, tape both the fabric and the design onto a sunny window or light box.

Tissue-paper method: Trace the design onto tissue paper with a pencil. Pin or baste the tissue paper onto the fabric and stitch the design through the paper onto the fabric. As each design section is completed, gently tear away the tissue paper. When finished, use tweezers to pick out any remaining tissue-paper bits left behind. This is a good method if using a textured fabric or felt.

Stick-N-Washaway by Pellon: This is a printer-ready sheet that eliminates the need for directly marking the fabric. Simply print the design on the sheet, remove its paper backing, and adhere the printed sheet to the top surface of the fabric. Stitch the design onto the sheet and fabric, and when the stitching is complete, wash away the sheet in water of any temperature. First, test the product in your printer before beginning to make sure the ink washes away with the sheet. All of the samples in this book were prepared with this method.

STITCHING

Now that you have gathered all the tools and materials needed and you've transferred your design to fabric, it's time to start stitching! Cut a length of thread 18" to 30" (45.5 cm to 76 cm). If you're new to embroidery, keep the thread on the shorter end of this range to avoid frustrating knots and tangles.

tip

To press your embroidery, first, cover the ironing board with a thick terry towel to avoid flattening the embroidery stitches. Iron the embroidery on the wrong side, using a pressing cloth and iron temperature appropriate for the fabric and thread used.

Next, secure the thread to the fabric. There are two ways to do this.

Simple knot: Make a small knot at one end of the thread. Cut the tail close to the knot. Start with the needle under the fabric, then bring it through the fabric at a starting point. The knot will be on the back of the fabric.

Waste knot: Make a good-sized knot at the end of the thread and insert the needle from the right side and within the area that will eventually be covered by the stitching. Work several elements of the design, covering and securing the thread on the back of the work at the same time. Then carefully cut off the knot.

When you're ready to end the working thread, stop with the thread and needle at the back of the fabric. Stitch through the backs of previously worked stitches for about 1" (2.5 cm), then stitch through those same stitches in the opposite direction. Cut the thread. The stitches will be secure with no knot to form a bump!

Remember to avoid leaving thread tails of any length on the back of the stitched piece, and do not carry stitching threads across unworked fabric areas. Keep the design backs tidy.

STITCH GUIDE

To create all the designs in this book, you'll need to know a variety of stitches. You can take some time to learn all the stitches that follow. Or learn the basics (such as backstitch, French knot, satin stitch, and stem stitch) and then refer back to this section for any special stitches used in a particular design.

✕ BACKSTITCH

Backstitch is an outlining stitch, producing a solid line that will easily bend around curves when the stitches are kept short.

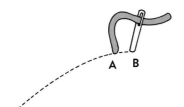
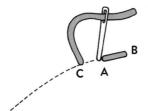
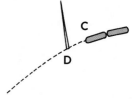

1 Bring the needle up at A, one stitch length from the start of the design line, and down at B at the beginning of the line.

2 Bring the needle up at C, one stitch length ahead of A, and down in the hole previously made by A.

3 Bring the needle up at D, making sure to maintain the same stitch length as before, and down at C. Continue in this stitching pattern of back one stitch and ahead two stitches.

✕ BASKET STITCH

Basket stitch is a good fill stitch when working between two lines, as for a branch or stem. The crisscross design adds texture and interest.

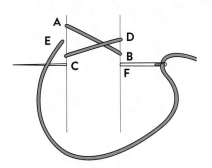 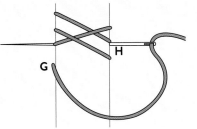 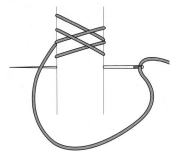

1 Bring the needle up at A and down at B, on the opposite edge and below the level of A. Bring the needle up at C, directly across from B on the opposite edge. Insert the needle down at D, above B, and up at E, between A and C. Insert the needle down at F.

2 Bring the needle up at G and down at H.

3 Continue to fill the space with crisscross diagonal stitches. If background fabric is visible between the stitches, it is called an **open basket stitch**, and if no fabric is visible, it's called a **closed basket stitch**.

- -

✕ BULLION STITCH

A bullion stitch is a stitch that can be used individually or grouped to form a filling.

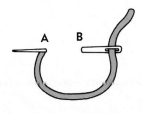 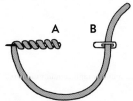 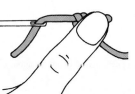

1 Bring the needle up at A and down at B, and then up at A again. Do not pull the needle through the fabric.

2 Wrap the working thread counterclockwise around the point of the needle five or six times or enough times to cover the distance between A and B.

3 Place your thumb on the wrapped threads to hold them in place and gently pull the needle through the wraps, taking care not to disturb them.

4 Insert the needle down at B and continue to gently pull the working thread until the bullion stitch lies flat.

✄ BUTTONHOLE STITCH

Buttonhole stitch is an edging stitch that can also be worked as an outline. The stitches are snugged up closely to each other. If they are spaced apart, then this stitch is known as the **blanket stitch**.

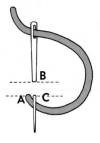

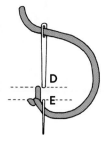

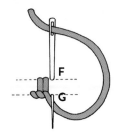

1 Bring the needle up at A and down at B, above and slightly to the right of A; bring the needle up at C, directly below B, keeping the working thread under the needle.

2 Tighten the thread to complete the stitch. Insert the needle down at D and up at E, directly below D, again with the thread under the needle.

3 Continue working stitches, keeping the stitch height and spacing as even as possible.

✄ CHAIN STITCH

Chain stitch can be used as an outline stitch or worked in rows as a lacy filling. It is made by working a series of connected looped stitches.

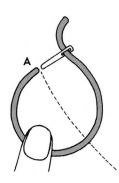

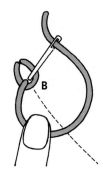

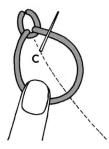

1 Bring the needle up at A; hold the thread down with your thumb and insert the needle down through the same hole.

2 Bring the needle up at B, inside the thread loop, and pull the thread gently to form a small loop. Insert the needle back down in the hole at B.

3 Bring the needle up at C to complete the next loop in the chain.

4 Finish the final loop with a small tack-down stitch; note that a single loop held down with the tack-down stitch is called **detached chain or lazy daisy stitch** (page 17).

✂ COLONIAL KNOT

Somewhat similar to a French knot (page 16), a colonial knot is made by wrapping the thread around the needle in a figure-eight pattern.

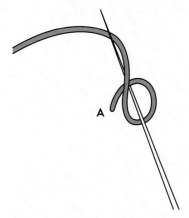 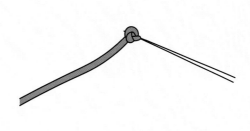

1 Bring the needle up at A and wrap the thread around the tip of the needle in a figure eight.

2 Tighten the thread around the needle and insert the needle down very close to A. Holding the wraps on the fabric surface, pull the thread through the knot and fabric. Tighten the knot again, if necessary.

✂ COUCHING

In couching, a separate thread, often decorative, is laid on top of the fabric and secured down with another separate thread. This can be accomplished with one or two thread colors or types.

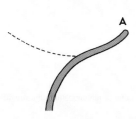 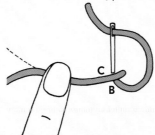 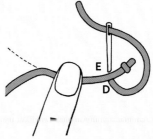

1 Bring the decorative thread up at A and lay it along the design line.

2 Hold this thread in position as you work, keeping it fairly taut. (Alternately, you can bring the needle down at the end of the design line, but do not secure it. This keeps the laid thread out of the way but allows you to tighten or loosen it throughout the process.) Bring the securing thread up at B and down at C on the opposite side of the laid thread.

3 Bring the needle up at D and down at E. The distance between the securing threads is determined by the effect you desire, usually about ¼" (6 mm) between C and B is a good starting point. Continue until the entire length of laid thread is couched down. Take the remaining end of the laid thread to the wrong side and secure both threads.

✕ FEATHER STITCH

Feather stitch can be used for outlines, borders, or fills.

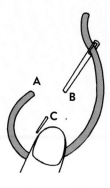 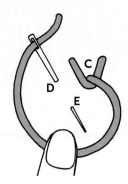 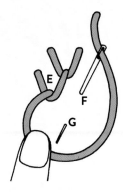

1 Bring the needle up at A and down at B (at the same height as A). Bring the needle up at C with the thread held below the needle. The distances between A, B, and C should be equidistant.

2 Insert the needle down at D and up at E, again keeping the thread under the needle. The distances between C, D, and E should also be equidistant.

3 Continue working in this way, always keeping the working thread under the needle. Secure the last loop with a tiny tack-down stitch.

- -

✕ FERN STITCH

Fern stitch is an easy stitch that creates a feathery effect, resembling a fern frond, and is ideal for plant leaves, borders, and line designs.

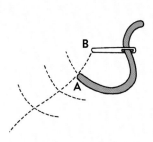 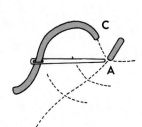 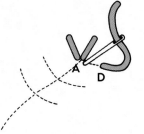 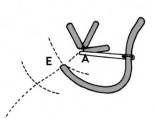

1 Bring the needle up at A and down at B.

2 Bring the needle up at C and down in the same hole as A.

3 Bring the needle up at D and down in the same hole as A. This completes a single fern stitch.

4 Bring the needle up at E and down in the same hole as A. Continue in this way to complete a stitch line.

✕ FISHBONE STITCH

Fishbone stitch is a fill stitch that is ideal for leaf and petal shapes. The stitches interweave at the center line, creating an appearance of a fish skeleton, if spaces are created between the lateral stitches.

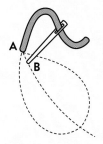 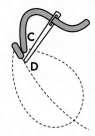 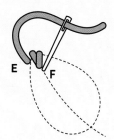 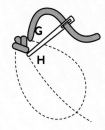

1 Bring the needle up at A and down at B, making a small straight stitch along the center line.

2 Bring the needle up at C at the left edge of the shape and down at D, slightly overlapping the base of the first stitch and at the center line.

3 Bring the needle up at E at the right edge of the shape and down at F, again overlapping the base of the previous stitch.

4 Bring the needle up at G and down at H. Cover the entire design shape in this way. The stitches can be either tightly grouped together so there are no gaps between them or spaced apart.

✕ FLY STITCH

Fly stitch can be used singly, as a scattered filling, in rows as a border, or as a close filling. The tack-down stitch that secures the thread loop can be short to resemble a V or long to resemble a Y.

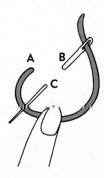 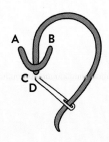

1 Bring the needle up at A, hold the thread loop down and insert the needle down at B, a little to the right and level with A. Bring the needle up at C, below and halfway between A and B, keeping the thread under the needle.

2 Tighten the thread and insert the needle down at D to make a small tack-down stitch.

⋈ FRENCH KNOT

French knots can be worked singly, in rows, or grouped together to create a textured surface.

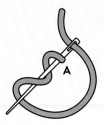

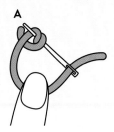

1 Bring the needle up at A and wrap the thread counterclockwise once or twice around the needle.

2 Holding the wraps firmly, insert the needle down adjacent to A.

3 Holding the wraps against the needle and fabric, pull the thread through the wraps and tighten the knot. If you wish the knot to be larger, add more thread strands. However, do not make more wraps, causing the knot to fall over and resemble a comma rather than a spherical knot.

⋈ LATTICE STITCH

Lattice stitch, also known as **trellis square filling**, creates a grid of straight stitches.

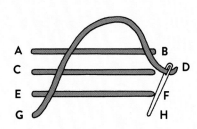

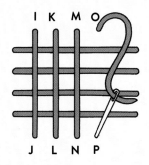

1 Sew rows of evenly spaced horizontal stitches over the area to be covered. They should lie smoothly against the fabric without pulling or being loose.

2 Sew the vertical stitches, also spaced equally apart. If your stitches are long, work small tack-down stitches at the thread intersections for stability.

✄ LAZY DAISY STITCH

Lazy daisy, or **detached chain stitch**, can be worked separately, in a line, or clustered. Here, four individual lazy daisy stitches are placed in a circle to form a flower shape, but any arrangement can be stitched.

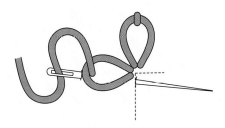 

1 Following the chain stitch instructions (page 12), make a detached chain stitch for the top petal. Sew a second petal to the left of the first and around a central point.

2 Continue around, forming the bottom petal and the petal on the right.

✄ LEAF STITCH

Leaf stitch is an open filling stitch with an interwoven central area that makes it ideal for stitching foliage.

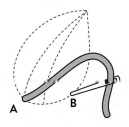 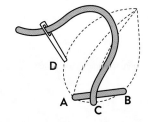 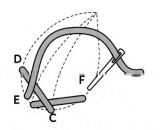 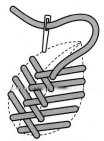

1 Bring the needle up at A and down at B to form a slanting stitch.

2 Bring the needle up at C, a short distance to the right of A, and down at D.

3 Bring the needle up at E, at the edge of the shape, and down at F, crossing stitching line CD.

4 Continue this sequence, working evenly spaced stitches on alternate sides to fill the entire shape.

✂ LONG AND SHORT SATIN STITCH

Long and short stitch is a variation of the satin stitch (page 19) and is quite often the main stitch used to solidly fill in a medium to large design area. This stitch requires a little practice to accomplish well.

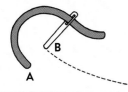 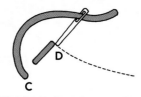 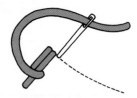

1 Bring the needle up at A and down at B at the outer edge of the design area.

2 Bring the needle up at C and down at D; note that this is a longer stitch and is stitched tightly against the first stitch.

3 Repeat these two short and long stitches to the end of the row or around a shape.

For all subsequent rows, bring the needle up a stitch length below the previous row and down through the base of the stitch above this row. Work all of these stitches the same length.

- -

✂ RHODES STITCH

Rhodes stitch makes a small multi-stitched, textured square that can be worked in different sizes. This is considered a counted thread stitch and is typically done on an evenweave fabric, which has the same number of stitches horizontally and vertically. If you're sewing on a regular cotton fabric, you can draw a square on the fabric with a fabric pen to guide your stitches.

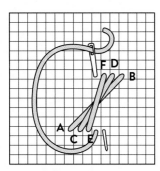 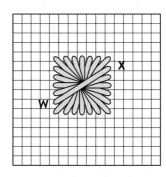

1 Bring the needle up at A at the lower left corner of the square and down six canvas strands above and to the right at B at the opposite corner. Bring needle up at C and down at D, up at E and down at F, traveling around the square.

2 The last stitch will be W to X.

✄ RUNNING STITCH

Running stitch is the simplest of all embroidery stitches.

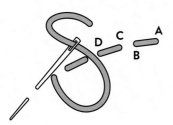

1 Starting at the right-hand end of the design line, bring the needle up at A and down at B. Bring needle up at C and down at D. Continue to sew all the stitches and gaps of equal length.

✄ SATIN STITCH

Satin stitch is a popular filling stitch consisting only of straight stitches. It takes a little practice to make the stitched surface smooth and the edges even, but this stitch is invaluable.

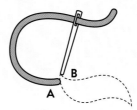

1 Bring the needle up at A and down at B, working from edge to edge of the design.

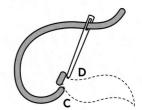

2 Bring the needle up at C and down at D. Continue working across the shape in this way, placing the stitches very close together so that no background fabric shows. Keep the edges of the shape even and neat.

✄ SEED STITCH

Seed stitch is a random arrangement of very short straight stitches and is excellent for filling areas quickly.

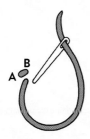

1 Bring the needle up at A and down at B, making a small straight stitch. Then bring the needle up a short distance away and make another stitch of the same length but at a different angle. Continue to fill the design area.

✕ SMYRNA CROSS-STITCH

The Smyrna cross-stitch, or **double cross-stitch**, consists of an upright cross-stitch sewn on top of a regular cross-stitch, forming a star pattern.

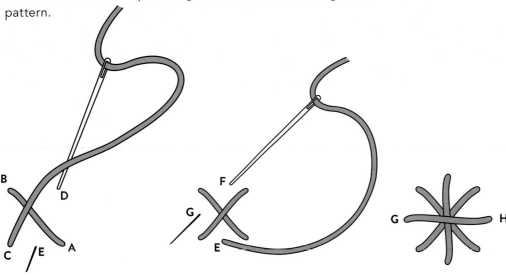

1 Sew the regular cross-stitch, going from A to B to C to D. Start the upright cross-stitch at E.

2 Bring the needle down at F and up at G.

3 Insert the needle down at H.

✕ SPLIT STITCH

Split stitch is an outline stitch that resembles a small chain stitch.

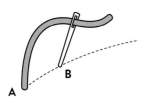

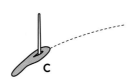

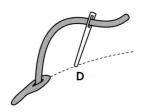

1 Bring the needle up at A and down at B.

2 Bring the needle up at C, piercing the thread of the previous stitch.

3 Insert the needle down at D to form the next stitch. Then bring the needle up to pierce the stitch just worked. Make all the stitches the same length and pierce them at the same point to create an even outline.

✂ STEM STITCH

Stem stitch is a popular outlining stitch. If you hold the thread above rather than below the line of stitching, the stitch is then called an **outline stitch**.

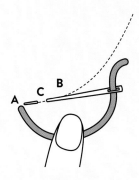 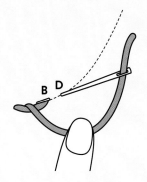 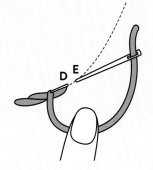

1 Bring the needle up at A, at the start of the design line, and down at B, holding the thread below the stitching line. Bring the needle up at C, midway between A and B.

2 Tighten the thread to complete the first stitch. Hold the working thread below the stitching line again and insert the needle down at D and up in the same hole as B.

3 Insert the needle down at E and up at D. Continue to make each stitch the same length.

✂ STRAIGHT STITCH

Straight stitch, a simple stitch of varying lengths, can be used singly or scattered to fill an area.

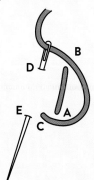

1 Bring the needle up at A and down at B. Bring the needle up at C and down at D. Continue to make straight stitches in any desired direction and length.

✂ WHIPPED BACKSTITCH

One way to embellish a backstitch or running stitch is to add another stitch. Here, a second thread is whipped around each backstitch, which may be of the same or a contrasting color.

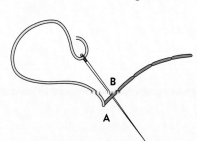 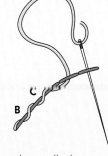

1 Backstitch (page 10) a design line. Using a second thread, bring the needle out at A and pass the needle downward and under the stitch between A and B without piercing the fabric.

2 Pass the needle downward and under the stitch between B and C, again without piercing the fabric. Continue in this way until all of the backstitches are whipped with the second thread.

the DESIGNS

A line is just a line. That line can be bent and shaped, stretched and pulled into something new. The shape of that line and how it connects to other lines has the power to create meaning, emotion, a memory, or a representation of something familiar. These are my lines; they have been shaped by my hand into animals and illustrations. Even when the lines are complete and the image is formed, it is still just a collection of lines on a sheet of paper. By using these lines as a road map for your handwork, they become something more; they become tactile and three-dimensional. Through stitching, they have color and personality.

These illustrations are some of my favorites that I have done over the years. I come back to them again and again. Most of the illustrations are of animals. Animals fascinate me. I have spent countless hours watching squirrels chase each other up and down trees. I have peered through aquarium glass while sea horses float eerily through their habitats, and I have looked my own dog in the eyes, dying to know what she is thinking. We personify animals in an effort to understand them better through our own lens, always aware that we will never really know what that inner dialogue is. Therein lies the magic of the mysterious animal kingdom and why so much of my work is centered on this theme.

DOUBLE BUNNY

A pair of mirrored bunnies hide among satin-stitch flowers and chain-stitch foliage. Working with light and darker shades of green give extra dimension to the leaves, tucking the bunnies deeper into the design. It's a game of hide-and-seek with stitching.

THREAD

Anchor 88

Anchor 118

Anchor 280

Anchor 281

Anchor 1070

STITCHES

Backstitch **(PAGE 10)**

Chain stitch **(PAGE 12)**

French knot **(PAGE 16)**

Satin stitch **(PAGE 19)**

Stem or outline stitch **(PAGE 21)**

Stitched by **ELISE BAEK**

COLOR PLACEMENT GUIDE

See CD for full-size pattern. Actual size is approximately 5¾" × 6¾" (14.5 cm × 17 cm).

1 Keep satin stitches as straight, close, and even as possible for the most impact.

2 The bunnies are almost hidden when stitched in a light purple backstitch. Use a more dense stitch or fill the forms to give the bunnies a stronger presence.

3 Use small chain stitch for a textured outline for foliage.

CHIPMUNK

This little rascal traverses tree branches with claws made of detached buttonhole stitch. There is a glint of mischief in his eye made with a single-strand French knot, while lazy daisy petals fluff out his tail.

THREAD

Anchor 1

Anchor 204

Anchor 206

Anchor 278

Anchor 280

Anchor 924

Anchor 1041

STITCHES

Backstitch **(PAGE 10)**

Buttonhole stitch variation **(PAGE 12)**

Fly stitch **(PAGE 15)**

French knot **(PAGE 16)**

Lazy daisy stitch **(PAGE 17)**

Satin stitch **(PAGE 19)**

Split stitch **(PAGE 20)**

Stem or outline stitch **(PAGE 21)**

Stitched by **CAROLINE DAIGLE**

COLOR PLACEMENT GUIDE
See CD for full-size pattern. Actual size is approximately 8" × 6¼" (20 cm × 16 cm).

DESIGNER INSIGHT

For added sparkle, Caroline suggests using beads and crystals for the stamens of the large flower.

1 Use fly stitches for the squiggles on the flower petals.

   For the stamens around the flower center, use two strands of one color floss to make straight stitches, then repeat using one strand of a different color floss.

2 For the nose, use satin stitches but make the bottom tip the pivot point for the stitches.

   Use a single-wrap French knot for the eye. All the others are double French knots, meaning the floss is wrapped around the needle twice.

3 Make the claws with detached buttonhole stitch. The detached buttonhole stitch is achieved by coming up at A and down at B (the distance of the chipmunk's toe) and up at A or a thread or two away from A (see Stitch Guide). Keeping this top loose thread taut but not so tight as to gather the fabric, sew tight buttonhole stitches around this thread, pushing the stitches tightly against one another to thoroughly cover the loose thread. Take the needle down at B and secure the thread on fabric back.

OWL

Wise beyond his years, this young colorful owl loves the night life but knows when it's time to turn in. You'll be wise to make use of French knots as polka dots to fill his body with texture quickly and effectively.

THREAD	STITCHES
Anchor 31	Backstitch **(PAGE 10)**
Anchor 178	Chain stitch **(PAGE 12)**
Anchor 280	Fishbone stitch **(PAGE 15)**
Anchor 302	French knot **(PAGE 16)**
Anchor 329	Lazy daisy stitch **(PAGE 17)**
Anchor 1070	Long and short satin stitch variation **(PAGE 18)**
Anchor 1089	Satin stitch **(PAGE 19)**
	Split stitch **(PAGE 20)**
	Stem or outline stitch **(PAGE 21)**

stitched by **REBECCA J. VENTON**

COLOR PLACEMENT GUIDE
See CD for full-size pattern. Actual size is approximately 4¾" × 8¼" (12 cm × 21 cm).

DESIGNER INSIGHT

Rebecca used three strands of thread for all the stitches in the owl for a very consistent bold look.

1 Form the contrasting lines in the owl eyes with split stitches. Lazy daisy stitches are perfect for holes in the beak.

2 Use a variation of the long and short satin stitch to add interest and texture.

3 Use satin stitches in bright blue around the eyes and in pink and yellow here on the tail to resemble feathers.

FLORAL SPRAY

Whimsical hand-embroidered creatures need flora just as magical as they are. In this sprig, you play with combining floss colors in a single stitch, adding interest to French knots. Woodgrain fabric is the perfect accent, too, giving this design a solid base.

THREAD	STITCHES
Anchor 31	Backstitch **(PAGE 10)**
Anchor 45	Blanket stitch **(SEE BUTTONHOLE STITCH, PAGE 12)**
Anchor 280	Chain stitch **(PAGE 12)**
Anchor 302	Feather stitch **(PAGE 14)**
Anchor 323	French knot **(PAGE 16)**
Anchor 330	Lazy daisy stitch **(PAGE 17)**
Anchor 1041	Satin stitch **(PAGE 19)**
Anchor 1070	Straight stitch **(PAGE 21)**

stitched by **ANNETTE MILLARD**

COLOR PLACEMENT GUIDE
See CD for full-size pattern. Actual size is
approximately 7½" × 9¼" (19 cm × 23.5 cm).

DESIGNER INSIGHT

To get the textured look of the branches, Annette outlined the branches in chain stitch and then filled in the branches with feather stitch.

1 Add depth to the design by using several colors of floss for some stitches. Use gray and turquoise for some French knots and pink and burgundy for others.

2 To fill in the flowers, use a large lazy daisy stitch with a tack-down stitch on each side.

DRAGONFLIES

This pair of dragonflies circle each other, as if dancing in the air, as they race from cattails to lily pads. Their fanciful wings and tails identify them, but who is whom is up to you.

THREAD

Anchor 188

Anchor 206

Anchor 253

Anchor 255

Anchor 302

Anchor 873

J. & P. Coats 03039

J. & P. Coats 00173

STITCHES

Backstitch **(PAGE 10)**

French knot **(PAGE 16)**

Satin stitch **(PAGE 19)**

Split stitch **(PAGE 20)**

Stem or outline stitch **(PAGE 21)**

Stitched by **JESSE COTTRELL**

COLOR PLACEMENT GUIDE

See CD for full-size pattern. Actual size is approximately 7½" × 9½" (19 cm × 24 cm).

1 Use a split stitch to outline the upper dragonfly's wings.

2 Vary the size of the French knots by varying the number of threads used. Outline the wing in backstitch.

3 Make the heads focal points of the design by stitching them with satin stitch.

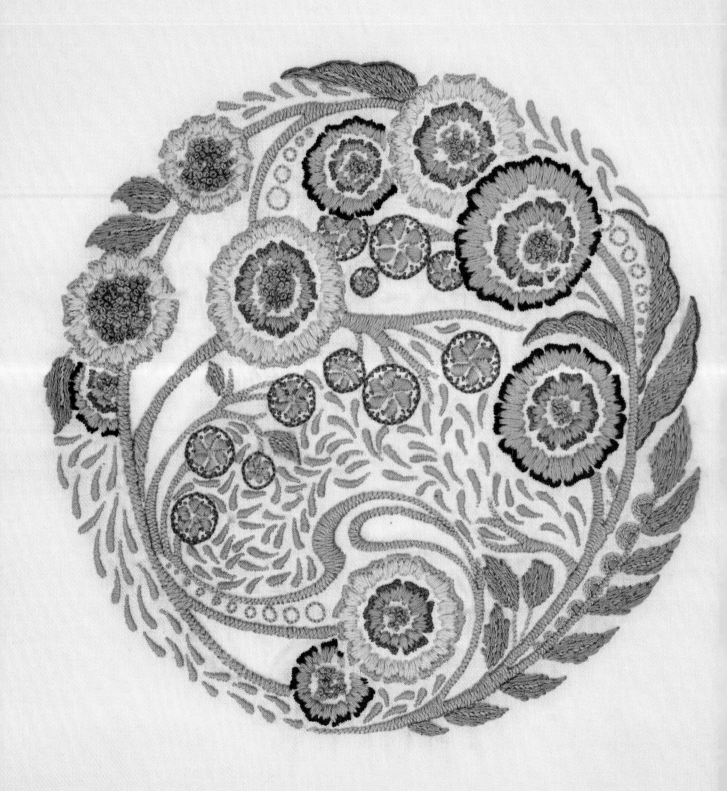

TOPIARY

- -

Tightly packed basket stitches are the secret to the unique texture and solid foundation the teal branches give this floral topiary. From them spring thread-painted flowers made lifelike with long and short satin stitches in two tones.

THREAD

Anchor 26

Anchor 27

Anchor 35

Anchor 45

Anchor 204

Anchor 280

Anchor 306

STITCHES

Backstitch **(PAGE 10)**

Basket stitch **(PAGE 11)**

Colonial knot **(PAGE 13)**

Couching **(PAGE 13)**

Long and short satin stitch variation **(PAGE 18)**

Satin stitch **(PAGE 19)**

Seed stitch **(PAGE 19)**

Split stitch **(PAGE 20)**

Stem or outline stitch **(PAGE 21)**

Stitched by **ANGELA ZOLNER**

COLOR PLACEMENT GUIDE
See CD for full-size pattern. Actual size is approximately 7½" × 7½" (19 cm × 19 cm).

DESIGNER INSIGHT

The inner and outer rows of each flower are a variation on the long and short satin stitch; Angela made the lengths random for a realistic floral effect. This is a thread-painting technique.

1 Use different-size knots and random color arrangements to add texture and interest to the center of the flowers.

2 Add texture to the branches with basket stitch.

3 Use couching stitch to outline one side of the large leaves.

OCTO

Gradient cephalopods spend their days slinking through coral reefs. This octopus has taken on the coral color of his surroundings, but in your whimsical world he could be any shade. Have fun using chain stitch and stem stitch together along the outlines of his tangled limbs.

THREAD	STITCHES
Anchor 33	Backstitch **(PAGE 10)**
Anchor 328	Chain stitch **(PAGE 12)**
Anchor 831	French knot **(PAGE 16)**
Anchor 1011	Long and short satin stitch variation **(PAGE 18)**
Anchor 1098	Satin stitch **(PAGE 19)**
	Stem or outline stitch **(PAGE 21)**

Stitched by **NICHOLE VOGELSINGER**

COLOR PLACEMENT GUIDE

See CD for full-size pattern. Actual size is approximately 6½" × 6¼" (16.5 cm × 16 cm).

1   Add movement and dimension to the stem-stitch outline by pairing it with a backstitch or chain-stitch outline in a lighter shade of floss.

2   Use a long and short satin-stitch variation to fill in an area with an interesting texture.

3   Backstitch to outline the suction cups and add a few satin stitches to fill in the centers.

OCEAN PONY

- -

Free from life in an aquarium, this pretty ocean pony can flutter his fins to anywhere he chooses. Use Rhodes stitch for an interesting bubble effect, while changing up the number of floss threads you use will easily change French knot sizes.

THREAD	STITCHES
Anchor 274	French knot **(PAGE 16)**
Anchor 848	Rhodes stitch variation **(PAGE 18)**
Anchor 850	Satin stitch **(PAGE 19)**
Anchor 851	Straight stitch **(PAGE 21)**
Anchor 1092	Whipped backstitch **(PAGE 21)**

Stitched by **EMILY VARDEMAN**

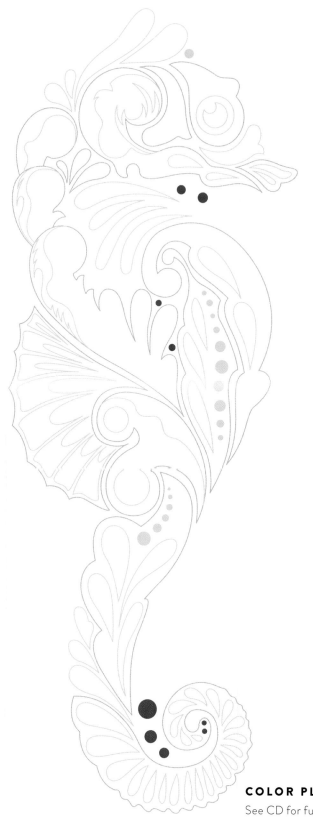

COLOR PLACEMENT GUIDE
See CD for full-size pattern. Actual size is
approximately 3¼" × 9" (8 cm × 23 cm).

1 Use six strands of thread for the largest French knots and three or fewer for the smaller knots.

2 Whipped backstitch adds movement and interest to the outline of the sea horse. Backstitch with a darker color and whipstitch with a lighter color.

3 Work Rhodes stitch in a circle to add great depth and texture to bubbles.

DEER

This majestic deer isn't as difficult to stitch as he might appear. Once you've stitched the foundation of a particular area, return with a single contrasting dark thread to add fine-line details. It's that small detail that has major impact.

THREAD	STITCHES
Anchor 31	French knot **(PAGE 16)**
Anchor 40	Lazy daisy stitch **(PAGE 17)**
Anchor 300	Satin stitch **(PAGE 19)**
Anchor 303	Split stitch **(PAGE 20)**
Anchor 387	Stem or outline stitch **(PAGE 21)**
Anchor 900	Straight stitch **(PAGE 21)**
Anchor 1041	
Anchor 1074	

stitched by **CHARLENE HEARST**

COLOR PLACEMENT GUIDE

See CD for full-size pattern. Actual size is approximately 5¾" × 9½" (14.5 cm × 24 cm).

1 Use straight stitches and one strand of floss over satin stitches to add dimension.

2 Create interest and texture in the antlers by using a mix of satin stitch for fill, split stitch for outlines, and straight stitch and French knots for details.

3 Use French knots to form the centers of the large flowers and for detail at the end of each petal.

DUCK

- -

Skimming smoothly across the surface of the water, this cabbage rose duck is a sight to see. Her grace comes with patience, stitching each rose with just two strands of floss for a finished look as sleek as feathers.

THREAD

Anchor 28

Anchor 31

Anchor 278

Anchor 279

Anchor 387

Anchor 1020

STITCHES

Chain stitch **(PAGE 12)**

French knot **(PAGE 16)**

Lazy daisy stitch **(PAGE 17)**

Leaf stitch **(PAGE 17)**

Satin stitch **(PAGE 19)**

Seed stitch **(PAGE 19)**

Smyrna cross-stitch **(PAGE 20)**

Split stitch **(PAGE 20)**

Stem or outline stitch **(PAGE 21)**

stitched by **ELIZABETH HILL**

COLOR PLACEMENT GUIDE

See CD for full-size pattern. Actual size is approximately 7¾" × 9¼" (19.5 cm × 23.5 cm).

DESIGNER INSIGHT

Elizabeth used satin stitch for all the cabbage roses, using two strands of floss. She needed two skeins of the light pink floss to complete the design.

1 Use Smyrna cross-stitch to form the berries.

2 Contrast the dense cabbage roses with lazy daisy flowers and leaf-stitch leaves.

HORSES

Rearing horses are given lifelike texture throughout their bodies and manes with split stitch. They're set against twisting vines and floral accents, ready to frolic among satin-stitch thistles.

THREAD	STITCHES
Anchor 45	Backstitch **(PAGE 10)**
Anchor 85	Satin stitch **(PAGE 19)**
Anchor 87	Seed stitch **(PAGE 19)**
Anchor 185	Split stitch **(PAGE 20)**
Anchor 1041	Stem or outline stitch **(PAGE 21)**
Anchor 1076	

Stitched by **PAT SMITH**

COLOR PLACEMENT GUIDE

See CD for full-size pattern. Actual size is approximately 7¾" × 9" (19.5 cm × 23 cm).

1 Backstitch can be used as a fill. Backstitch to outline the large flowers, then use the stitch in a different color floss to fill them.

2 Use split stitch as a fill on the horse to give texture to the coat and mane.

3 Use satin stitch to fill in the small pink flowers and the leaves.

FLY FROG KING

Nestled in the belly of the mighty Fly Frog King is a sweet little fly that uses stem stitch as a filler rather than the usual outline. The design is buzzing with other charming details—from the full bright wings to the curl of the legs ready to leap.

THREAD

Anchor 152

Anchor 208

Anchor 254

Anchor 266

Anchor 387

Anchor 1068

Anchor 1092

STITCHES

French knot **(PAGE 16)**

Lattice stitch with tack-down stitches **(PAGE 16)**

Lazy daisy stitch **(PAGE 17)**

Satin stitch **(PAGE 19)**

Split stitch **(PAGE 20)**

Stem or outline stitch **(PAGE 21)**

stitched by **JANICE SIMMONS**

COLOR PLACEMENT GUIDE

See CD for full-size pattern. Actual size is approximately 7¾" × 9" (19.5 cm × 23 cm).

1. Outline the wings in stem stitch and use split stitch to add some of the detail.

2. Use lattice stitch for an interesting fill that isn't too dense. Add a tiny tack-down stitch at each thread intersection for stability.

3. While stem stitch is usually used for outlining, rows of it can be used as a fill. Use it to fill the bug's body.

4. Use two rows of stem stitch to outline the frog's face, using two strands of floss in one row and three strands in the second row.

BUTTERFLY

- -

From antennae to wing tip, simple touches make for beautiful details in this powerful butterfly. Fern stitch, colonial knots, and satin stitches that alternate directions are used to achieve the effects.

THREAD

Anchor 28

Anchor 31

Anchor 45

Anchor 303

STITCHES

Backstitch (**PAGE 10**)

Bullion stitch (**PAGE 11**)

Colonial knot (**PAGE 13**)

Couching (**PAGE 13**)

Fern stitch (**PAGE 14**)

French knot (**PAGE 16**)

Satin stitch (**PAGE 19**)

Split stitch (**PAGE 20**)

Stitched by **ANGELA ZOLNER**

COLOR PLACEMENT GUIDE

See CD for full-size pattern. Actual size is approximately 7½" × 8" (19 cm × 20 cm).

DESIGNER INSIGHT

For a touch of realism, Angela used fern stitch to simulate the fine hairs on a butterfly's antennae.

1 Alternate the direction of the satin stitch for each section. Couch down the satin stitches running perpendicular to the motif's length to help these stitches curve with the pattern.

2 Keep the circle elements light by using backstitch for the outline and a colonial knot for the dot.

FLOWERS

Packing stitches tightly together makes for a dense design with incredible texture and detail. You'll be running your hand over the surface of this embroidery and leaning close to it as if its scent is as sweet as a rose when you're done.

THREAD

Anchor 35

Anchor 40

Anchor 253

Anchor 269

Anchor 397

Anchor 1041

Anchor 1094

STITCHES

Backstitch **(PAGE 10)**

French knot **(PAGE 16)**

Satin stitch **(PAGE 19)**

Straight stitch **(PAGE 21)**

Stitched by **JENNA J. BEEGLE**

COLOR PLACEMENT GUIDE

See CD for full-size pattern. Actual size is approximately 7¼" × 7¾" (18.5 cm × 19.5 cm).

1 Add texture to the large flower center with French knots.

2 Fill the flower petals with satin stitches of varying lengths.

3 Use rows of closely stitched backstitches in the leaves to contrast with the satin-stitched flowers.

LARGE BUNNY

This large bunny is posed ready to dash. Fueled by the fanciful flowers that fill his frame, they'll be no stopping him. The tortoise might just lose the race this time.

THREAD	STITCHES
Anchor 54	French knot **(PAGE 16)**
Anchor 278	Lazy daisy stitch **(PAGE 17)**
Anchor 281	Long and short satin stitch variation **(PAGE 18)**
Anchor 323	Satin stitch **(PAGE 19)**
Anchor 1076	Stem or outline stitch **(PAGE 21)**

Stitched by **ELIZABETH HILL**

COLOR PLACEMENT GUIDE

See CD for full-size pattern. Actual size is approximately 6¼" × 8½" (16 cm × 21.5 cm).

DESIGNER INSIGHT

Elizabeth would normally select a linen-like fabric for embroidery, but she liked the lacy look of this tonal print. In addition, this was a dense design with a lot of detail, so she thought the close weave of the tonal print would be sturdier.

1 Use satin stitch to fill in the round flowers, leaves, and eyes.

2 The petaled flowers in this design are perfect for the lazy daisy stitch. Add a French knot in the center for a sweet flower. Use lazy daisy stitches for the claws, too.

3 Use either outline or stem stitch to outline the design.

FLOWER BEE

- -

Bumble bee and flower bud merge into one and take center stage in this dramatic motif. French knots line up in a well-choreographed routine around the Flower Bee for one showstopping design.

THREAD

Anchor 40

Anchor 206

Anchor 255

Anchor 303

Anchor 1096

Anchor 1098

STITCHES

Backstitch **(PAGE 10)**

Blanket stitch **(SEE BUTTONHOLE STITCH, PAGE 12)**

Chain stitch **(PAGE 12)**

Colonial knot **(PAGE 13)**

Fern stitch **(PAGE 14)**

Fishbone stitch **(PAGE 15)**

Fly stitch **(PAGE 15)**

French knot **(PAGE 16)**

Satin stitch **(PAGE 19)**

Straight stitch **(PAGE 21)**

Stitched by **NYDIA KEHNLE**

COLOR PLACEMENT GUIDE

See CD for full-size pattern. Actual size is approximately 7½" × 8¼" (19 cm × 21 cm).

1 Keep the radiating lines in the flower petals delicate with a single strand of floss and backstitch.

Stitching the center of the eyes with satin stitch allows them to pop off the aqua-colored fly stitches.

2 Vary the number of strands you use to vary the size of the French knots. Use one strand for the knots in the circle motif, two strands for the tips of the antennae, and three strands for the colonial knots in the border.

In the circle motif, couch the circumference of the small circle with two colors of thread.

3 Use one strand of floss for the fishbone stitch on the smallest leaves; use two strands for the larger leaves. Use fern stitch for the stems connecting the small leaves.

ELEPHANT

A regal elephant in a majestic headdress pulls you in with a deep stare in this captivating ombrê design. Shifting colors from darker shades of teal into pale blue and eventually golden yellows gives the look of movement to stable stitches.

THREAD

Anchor 185

Anchor 186

Anchor 188

Anchor 278

Anchor 295

Anchor 305

Anchor 387

STITCHES

Bullion stitch **(PAGE 11)**

Chain stitch **(PAGE 12)**

Fern stitch **(PAGE 14)**

Fly stitch **(PAGE 15)**

French knot **(PAGE 16)**

Lazy daisy stitch **(PAGE 17)**

Satin stitch **(PAGE 19)**

Split stitch **(PAGE 20)**

Stem or outline stitch **(PAGE 21)**

stitched by **HANNAH ROBINSON**

COLOR PLACEMENT GUIDE

See CD for full-size pattern. Actual size is approximately 7¾" × 9½" (19.5 cm × 24 cm).

1. Use French knots as a fill for strong visual impact.

2. Use fern stitch to add a light and lacy quality to the side feathers.

3. Add ridged texture to the top of the forehead piece with bullion stitch (in darkest teal).

RESOURCES

The products used to create the designs in this book can be found at your local fabric, embroidery, or craft store. Below are the manufacturers of the products used to create these designs, but feel free to substitute other products.

THREAD

Anchor
makeitcoats.com
Embroidery floss

J. & P. Coats
makeitcoats.com
Embroidery floss

FABRIC

FreeSpirit
freespiritfabrics.com
Tula Pink fabric

TRANSFER STABILIZER

Pellon
pellonprojects.com
Stick-N-Washaway

metric conversion chart

TO CONVERT	TO	MULTIPLY BY
Inches	Centimeters	2.54
Centimeters	Inches	0.4
Feet	Centimeters	30.5
Centimeters	Feet	0.03
Yards	Meters	0.9
Meters	Yards	1.1

ABOUT THE AUTHOR

Tula Pink is an American textile designer and quiltmaker with a dark sense of humor buried in a sea of print and patterns. She plays with images the way a poet plays with words, turning innocuous traditional designs into mischievous little critters. Her love affair with textiles began early, and an obsession with sewing soon followed. Several years and more than twenty fabric collections later, design is her true passion. Tula began quilting in an effort to use up her ever-growing stash of fabric so she could justify buying more. Twenty years later, she has a lot of quilts and more fabric than when she started. Visit Tula online at tulapink.com.

EVEN MORE GREAT
hand embroidery designs
ARE AT THE TIP OF YOUR NEEDLE
WITH THESE RESOURCES!

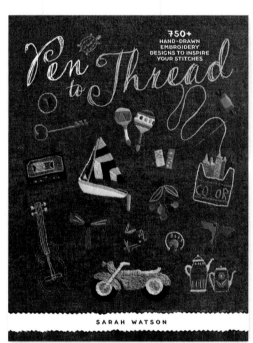

Modern Folk Embroidery

30 Contemporary Projects for
Folk Art Inspired Designs

NANCY NICHOLSON

978-1-44630-629-1
$22.99

Pen to Thread

750+ Hand-Drawn Embroidery
Designs to Inspire Your Stitches

SARAH WATSON

978-1-62033-952-7
$26.99

Fons&Porter

Available at ShopFonsandPorter.com or your local retailer